# LIVING FROM SOUL

*The SECRET to Living Your Authentic Self*

Dr. Eleanor Haspel-Portner

© 2025 ALL RIGHTS RESERVED.

Published by **Noble Sciences, LLC.**

No part of this book may be reproduced or transmitted in any form whatsoever, electronic, or mechanical, including photocopying, recording, or by any informational storage or retrieval system without the expressed written, dated and signed permission from the publisher and author.

LIMITS OF LIABILITY/DISCLAIMER OF WARRANTY:

The author and publisher of this book have used their best efforts in preparing this material. While every attempt has been made to verify the information provided in this book, neither the author nor the publisher assumes any responsibility for any errors, omissions, or inaccuracies.

The author and publisher make no representation or warranties with respect to the accuracy, applicability, or completeness of the contents of this book. They disclaim any warranties (expressed or implied), merchantability, or for any purpose. The author and publisher shall in no event be held liable for any loss or other damages, including but not limited to special, incidental, consequential, or other damages.

ISBN: 978-1-931053-23-5 (Paperback)
ISBN: 978-1-931053-24-2 (eBook)

# Dedication

*To all seekers of truth and their connection to the divine—*

*May you remember that you "Know what you Know because you Know it, and nobody can tell you that you don't Know it."*

*May you honor the sacred voice within that whispers your deepest truths, trust the divine guidance that flows through you, and live courageously from the spiritual core of who you truly are.*

*This work is offered in service to your journey of awakening to your own divinity and manifesting your highest potential in this world.*

# Foreword

It's hard to find words that truly honor the depth of transformation I've experienced through working with Dr. Eleanor Haspel-Portner, and yet, it's my privilege to try.

Since 2006, I've had the extraordinary opportunity to walk alongside Dr. Eleanor, supporting her in the development of her teachings, helping shape materials, co-creating classes, and bringing her vision to life in form and function. In the process, I have not only witnessed the profound depth and integrity of her work, but I have also been changed by it.

Living from Soul is not just another offering. It is the distilled essence of decades of insight, research, and profound spiritual wisdom. This body of work is both a guide and a mirror, revealing who we truly are beneath conditioning, beneath roles, and fear. Dr. Eleanor doesn't just teach from theory; she transmits lived wisdom that reaches straight to the heart. She does not just point the way; she activates something alive and essential within the very core of being.

For me, working with these tools and teachings has been a process of remembering, of reclaiming the parts of myself that were buried or forgotten. Dr. Eleanor's multidimensional approach awakened a knowing in me that words can't quite describe. It's the knowing that reorients your compass and changes your life.

This book is a gift. A profound invitation to return to yourself as a whole, empowered, and soul-aligned energetic being.

I offer this foreword with humility and gratitude, in honor of the sacred journey Dr. Eleanor so generously shares with us all. May this offering serve you as it has served me: as a beacon home.

Offered with Love and the Deepest Respect,
Cindy Smith ~ 2025

# Preface

When the Holy Spirit speaks to you and gives you a task, you don't have a lot of choice if you want to be conscious. This book emerged from such a divine directive—a calling that came through years of webinars, teachings, and countless conversations with seekers who, like me, knew there had to be more to human consciousness than what traditional psychology offered.

I've been a clinical psychologist for over fifty years, and in all that time, the pain I've witnessed most consistently was people not being recognized for who they knew themselves to be. They came to me carrying the weight of not being acknowledged for their true essence, their divine nature, their authentic self. This book is my response to that collective wound—a roadmap to who you are.

When you know what you know because you know it, nobody can tell you that you don't know it. I've said this thousands of times because it's the cornerstone of everything I teach. You were born whole. My statistical and clinical research on over 45,000 cases proves that you were complete by the time you were three months old, with your spiritual essence fully anchored in your being. Your parents' job was to honor that wholeness and teach you the integrity of being fully yourself. Unfortunately, most of us didn't receive that gift.

Instead, we were socialized into a world that focuses primarily on the Mental/Waking World—what you achieve, how smart you are, what school you attended, how you perform. Very little energy focuses on "What does your spirit want?" or "What's right for you to do in your life?" We internalize the lie that we exist only in conscious and unconscious states when, in reality, we function in multiple dimensions of time and space.

This book introduces you to the Four Worlds—Mental/Waking, Physical/Biological, Emotional/Angelic, and Spiritual/Archetypal—and shows you how to integrate them into an Integrated and unified field of consciousness. These aren't just concepts; they're living dimensions of your being that you can learn to navigate consciously. Life becomes play when you understand how to move fluidly between these worlds. It's your playground, and it's not so serious.

The material in these pages comes from decades of clinical work, extensive research in developmental psychology, and my journey of awakening, which began with a profound Kundalini experience in 1974. That experience provided me with a template for relationships, consciousness, and the multidimensional nature of human beings. It set me on a path that would eventually lead to the development of the Noble Energy Maps® and understanding how we are divinely designed to manifest our actual potential.

I want to be clear about something: you are not conditioned. You are socialized to your culture, but you are not conditioned. This distinction is crucial because conditioning implies an automated response that's hard to change, while socialization is simply learning the customs and practices of your environment. You have the power to choose what serves you and what doesn't.

Every single one of you reading this book has everything you need to reach a state called Self-Actualization. The question is: how do you get past your limitations? Consider overcoming your limitations by recognizing that you're a multidimensional being with access to spiritual intelligence, emotional wisdom, physical knowledge, and mental clarity. You're not meant to live compartmentalized—you're designed to live integrating all the worlds.

This book's exercises, insights, and practices serve as invitations to remember what you already know. Use them as tools for self-discovery, not as rules to follow. Make them your own. Color outside the lines. Trust your process more than any external authority, including me.

I've never worked a day in my life because I love what I do, and I do what I love. What I do isn't work for me—it's love. It's my contribution to the collective awakening happening on our planet. We're moving from third-dimensional reality into higher dimensions of consciousness, and we need guides for that journey. This book is one such guide.

As you read these pages, remember you're not trying to become someone new. You're trying to remember who you've always been. You're peeling away the layers that hide your divine self, the truth about who you are. And when you manifest that truth, what you can accomplish is unlimited.

The breath, every breath we take, breathes divinity into us. When the divine breathes you, everything lines up and flows, and you don't get tired because you're not using your energy. The divine frequency I invite you to remember is the state of being I want to help you reclaim.

Welcome to your journey home to yourself.

*Dr. Eleanor Haspel-Portner*

# TABLE OF CONTENTS

Foreword ......................................................................................... 5

Preface ............................................................................................ 6

Introduction: The Journey Begins ............................................... 11

**Part One: Understanding Your Multidimensional Nature** ................. 13

Chapter 1: The Architecture of Being - Your Four Worlds .................... 15

Chapter 2: The Mental/Waking World - Beyond the Mind .................... 18

Chapter 3: The Emotional/Angelic World - Transforming Energy ......... 20

Chapter 4: The Physical/Biological World - Honoring the Temple ........ 23

Chapter 5: The Spiritual/Archetypal - Your Divine Essence .................. 26

Chapter 6: The Integrated World - Living in Flow ................................ 29

**Part Two: Foundation Practices** ................................................ 33

Chapter 7: The Power of Breath and Movement ................................... 35

Chapter 8: Meditation and Sacred Presence ......................................... 38

Chapter 9: Dream Consciousness - Messages from Beyond ................... 41

**Part Three: Integration Practices** ............................................. 45

Chapter 10: Journaling for Transformation .......................................... 47

Chapter 11: Clean Questions and Authentic Communication ............... 50

Chapter 12: Gratitude as Transformation ............................................. 53

**Part Four: Living Your Truth** ..................................................... 57

Chapter 13: Manifesting from Your Soul .............................................. 59

Chapter 14: Navigating Relationships Authentically ............................ 62

Chapter 15: Self-Care as Spiritual Practice .......................................... 66

Chapter 16: Discovering Your Life Purpose ......................................... 69

**Part Five: Advanced Applications** ............................................................... 73

Chapter 17: Navigating Fear and Transformation ........................ 75

Chapter 18: Living Authentically in a Challenging World ...................... 79

Conclusion: The Journey Continues ............................................................ 83

Appendix A: Four Worlds Self-Assessment ................................................. 86

Appendix B: Daily Integration Practices...................................................... 90

Appendix C: Troubleshooting Common Challenges.................................. 94

About Dr. Eleanor............................................................................................ 99

Recommended Resources ........................................................................... 101

## INTRODUCTION

# THE JOURNEY BEGINS

This book emerges from the teachings and wisdom of Dr. Eleanor, a clinical psychologist, researcher, and spiritual guide with over five decades of experience. Throughout these pages, you'll discover a profound and integrative approach to understanding yourself as a multidimensional being living in Four Worlds. The Worlds are the Mental/Waking, Spiritual/Archetypal, Emotional/Angelic, Physical/Biological, and how to navigate and integrate them with grace and authenticity.

The journey to living from the soul begins with a fundamental truth: you are, at your core, a divine being living a human experience. Your essence—what Dr. Eleanor calls "the Soul"—remains constant and accurate, even as life's challenges and expectations of the Mental/Waking Life attempt to pull you away from your inner knowing and alignment. Dr. Eleanor documented her work scientifically on over 45,000 cases that she analyzed statistically and clinically. Dr. Eleanor's work and her development of Noble Energy Maps® remain the only scientifically documented spiritual system to date.

In these pages, you'll find concepts, transformative practices, personal stories, and pathways to reconnect with your authentic self across all dimensions of your existence. This work invites you to remember who you truly are, to release what does not serve you, and to live with full presence in the integrated flow of all Four Worlds.

As you read, allow yourself to feel the resonance of these words with your inner knowing. Dr. Eleanor often reminds us:

*"When you Know what you Know because you Know it, and nobody can tell you that you don't Know it, you are in alignment with your Soul."*

Welcome to the journey of Living from Soul.

# PART ONE:

## Understanding Your Multidimensional Nature

## CHAPTER 1

# THE ARCHITECTURE OF BEING - YOUR FOUR WORLDS

*"You are not just conscious or unconscious. You function in multiple dimensions in time and space. The more you learn the roadmap for yourself, the more you can navigate and interact with those worlds, the more dimensionality your life takes on, and the more robust you and your life are."*

A complex, magnificent architecture exists in the depths of your being—a multidimensional reality that transcends the simplistic view of consciousness as merely "conscious" and "unconscious." This architecture comprises Four Worlds that simultaneously exist within you: the Mental/Waking World, the Emotional/Angelic World, the Physical/Biological World, and the Spiritual/Archetypal World. And beyond these four exists a fifth—the Integrated World, where all dimensions harmonize and flow together.

The Mental/Waking World is where we typically function day-to-day. It's the reality plane of thinking, acting, and behaving. It's the world where you've been socialized to the norms and expectations of your culture. It's where you form concepts, create boundaries, make judgments, and interact with the "reality" you perceive around you.

The Emotional/Angelic World is the realm of feeling and transformation. It's where reactions arise—the joy, the pain, the anger, the love—and where these energies can either remain stuck as reactivity or transform into higher frequencies. The Emotional World connects to the Angelic World, where Creative Intelligence can elevate lower frequencies to higher expressions.

The Physical/Biological World is the body, the temple of your soul. It's the tangible vehicle through which you experience life. Often taken for granted, this world has its own intelligence, memory, and capacity for transformation. The Physical/Biological World operates autonomously, yet is deeply influenced by how you think, feel, and connect spiritually. The Physical/Biological World primarily functions beneath conscious awareness, as demonstrated in the Galvanic Skin Response used in lie detector tests. These tests confirm that Emotional responses occur before you become aware of them.

The Spiritual/Archetypal World is the unifying, integrative field of consciousness. It's the realm of your true essence, your divine nature. It's where you connect to your highest Knowing, intuition, and purpose. The Spiritual/Archetypal World isn't separate from the other Worlds—it flows through them, informing and enlivening them.

Most importantly, you simultaneously exist as an integrated being across all these worlds. When you feel fragmented, disconnected, or out of alignment, you often live primarily in one world while neglecting the others. True wholeness comes from recognizing the interplay of all dimensions and allowing them to harmonize.

As you understand this multidimensional architecture of your being, you open yourself to greater consciousness, freedom, and capacity to manifest your authentic self.

## Integration Practice: Four Worlds Daily Check-In

Begin developing your awareness of the Four Worlds with this simple practice. Several times throughout your day, pause and ask:

- Mental/Waking World: Am I in the right place, heading in the right direction?
- Emotional/Angelic World: What do I want to have happen now?

- Physical/Biological World: What do I know about my Physical state of being now?
- Spiritual/Archetypal World: What do I know now about _____?

*Notice which worlds you're naturally aware of and which you might be neglecting. This awareness is the first step toward integration.*

CHAPTER 2

# THE MENTAL/WAKING WORLD - BEYOND THE MIND

*"We've been told in this culture by the deep state that we're mental beings, and everything focuses on intellect. How smart are you? How much have you achieved? What school did you go to? How much education do you have, and how do you perform? There is very little energy put into 'what does your spirit want?'"*

The Mental/Waking World—your third-dimensional reality—is most likely where you've learned to exist primarily. It's the world of thinking, planning, judging, naming, categorizing, and social functioning. It's the world where you've been taught that your value comes from what you know, what you achieve, and how well you conform to external expectations.

But the Mental/Waking World, while necessary, was never meant to be your primary home. When you live predominantly in this dimension, you miss the richness, depth, and wisdom available through the other worlds. You become like a house with only one room occupied, while beautiful, spacious chambers remain unexplored.

In the Mental/Waking World, language becomes critically important. The words you use with others and in your self-talk carry frequencies that either empower or diminish you. When you speak from mental constructs alone, you often create limitations, barriers, and judgments that imprison you. You construct stories about who you are that may have little connection to your true essence.

The Mental/Waking World is where you often get stuck in the past or the future, missing the only moment that truly exists—the now. The Mental/Waking World is where you develop the habit of overthinking, overanalyzing, and creating scenarios that generate anxiety and fear rather than presence and flow.

The Mental/Waking World has tremendous gifts when properly understood and placed in appropriate relationships with the other worlds. It allows you to discern, articulate, plan, and manifest concretely. It enables you to communicate, build, and create structures that support your deeper purpose.

The key is recognizing that the Mental/Waking World is meant to be a servant, not a master. It is designed to take direction from your spiritual essence, not to override it. When the Mental/Waking World correctly aligns with your Spiritual/Archetypal nature, it becomes an extraordinary tool for expressing your authentic self in tangible ways.

## Transform Your Relationship with the Mental/Waking World

Begin to notice when you're overthinking, overanalyzing, or caught in mental loops.

- Become aware of the language you use internally and externally—does it uplift or diminish you?
- Practice returning to the present moment through breathing, sensory awareness, or simple physical movement.
- Ask yourself, "Is this thought/belief serving my highest good and authentic, aligned expression?"
- Before making decisions, check if you're operating solely from a Mental/Waking World construct or allowing your spiritual/archetypal knowing to guide your cognitive process.

*As you reorient your relationship with the Mental/Waking World, you'll discover it becomes a powerful ally in expressing your soul's purpose rather than an obstacle to it.*

CHAPTER 3

# THE EMOTIONAL/ANGELIC WORLD - TRANSFORMING ENERGY

> *"The Emotional/Angelic World is where you get reactive. I call it the Angelic World because when you clear all of the emotional baggage that comes with interactions and with playing in the Mental/Waking World, at that point, you become more like Jesus, all loving, all compassionate, and not reactive unless the reaction is in service of the higher self."*

The Emotional/Angelic World is both a blessing and a challenge on your journey toward wholeness. It is here that you experience the full spectrum of human feeling—from the depths of despair to the heights of ecstasy, from crippling fear to boundless courage, from smoldering anger to profound compassion.

What makes the Emotional/Angelic World unique is its transformative potential. Unlike the Mental/Waking World, which tends to categorize and judge emotions, or the Physical/Biological World, which simply registers emotions and reactions to your experiences as sensations, the Emotional/Angelic World offers you the opportunity to transmute lower-frequency emotions into their higher-frequency expressions.

Dr. Eleanor observed that emotional reactivity—those automatic, often unconscious responses triggered by people and circumstances—belongs primarily to the third-dimensional reality of the Mental/Waking and Physical/Biological Worlds. These reactions frequently stem from past conditioning, unhealed wounds, or misaligned perspectives.

When you learn to transform emotional reactivity, you enter what Dr. Eleanor calls the Angelic World—where emotions become clarified, purified, and elevated. In this dimension, emotions no longer control you; they inform, guide, and connect you to more profound truths.

The key insight about the Emotional/Angelic World is that it cannot transform itself. You can shift emotional energy, but only through spiritually connected awareness. When you attempt to process emotions purely through mental analysis or physical expression, you often remain stuck in cycles of reactivity. It's only by bringing a spiritual perspective to your emotions that true transformation occurs.

Practices such as meditation, prayer, breathwork, and conscious movement are powerful because they bridge emotional experience and spiritual understanding between the Emotional/Angelic and the Spiritual/Archetypal Worlds. They allow you to witness your emotions from a higher perspective, neither suppressing nor being consumed by them.

## The Emotional Transformation Process

When emotions arise, rather than immediately reacting or attempting to think your way through them, try this transformative approach:

- Acknowledge the emotion without judgment (you are not your emotion).
- Breathe deeply, creating space around the emotional energy.
- Ask, "What is this emotion trying to teach me? What wisdom does it contain?"
- Connect to your spiritual center, your divine essence, and radiate love, compassion, and understanding.
- Allow the emotion to transform in the light of your spiritual awareness.

Remember that emotions, in their essence, are simply energy in motion. They become problematic only when they get stuck, suppressed, or misinterpreted. Emotions become powerful allies in your journey toward authentic living when allowed to flow through the elevated awareness of your spiritual nature. Move your consciousness from the Mental/Waking and Physical/Biological Worlds, where you concretize emotions, to the Emotional/Angelic World, where love and compassion, as well as other aspects of Creative Intelligence, remain active and dominant.

*As Dr. Eleanor reminds us, "The Emotional/Angelic World is here to transform emotions into spirit." When you understand this profound truth, your emotional life becomes not an obstacle to overcome but a sacred pathway to your highest expression.*

## CHAPTER 4

# THE PHYSICAL/BIOLOGICAL WORLD - HONORING THE TEMPLE

*"Our body is complex. The brain, especially, is very complex. When we're sitting here, our spirit is active. Our body is active. We're breathing. Our emotions are active. We're in an Integrated World. We're not just in a Mental/Waking World with no spirit going on at that time; we're breathing, and our heart is beating. So, the Physical/Biological World is functioning actively, and most of the time, we're not paying attention to it or even thinking about it."*

The Physical/Biological World—your body—is the sacred vessel through which you experience all other dimensions of existence. However, in our culture, the body is often treated as separate from our spiritual nature, even as an obstacle to spiritual growth, rather than an essential part of it.

Your physical body exists as a miracle of divine engineering. It contains vast intelligence, processes billions of operations per second without conscious direction, and houses the energetic pathways through which your life force flows. The body remembers what the mind forgets, feels what the mind denies, and knows what the mind questions.

In the Noble Energy Maps® developed by Dr. Eleanor, the Physical/Biological World operates through a unique matrix of energy centers and channels. Interestingly, this matrix does not include the head centers (Crown and Ajna), suggesting that the physical body operates largely beyond the realm of Mental/Waking World control. However, it is not separate from these influences—the thoughts you think and the emotions you feel profoundly impact your physical well-being.

# Developing a Sacred Relationship with Your Body

One of the most critical practices for living authentically is cultivating a loving, respectful relationship with your physical body.

1. **Listen to the body's wisdom:**
   Your body communicates constantly through sensations, energy levels, and intuitive knowing. You gain access to profound guidance when you learn to listen to these messages rather than override them **with mental directives.**

2. **Honor the body's needs:**
   Rest when tired, eat when hungry, and move when stagnant. These simple alignments with your body's natural rhythms create a foundation for physical well-being and spiritual connection. By consciously directing your body, you are practicing mindful intentionality. The mind/body connection bridges the Mental/Waking, Physical/Biological, and Spiritual/Mental Worlds. By consciously using your Emotional/Angelic World to guide yourself into a spiritually aligned internal space, you activate your Creative Intelligence, building self-esteem and resilience.

3. **Speak kindly to your body:**
   Your language about and toward your body carries energetic frequencies. When you criticize your body or focus on perceived flaws, you create dissonance in your energy field. Practice speaking to your body with gratitude and love. Take a moment to look at yourself in a mirror and send love to yourself using empowering self-talk.

4. **Move in ways that integrate all worlds:**
   Practices like Tai Chi Gung, which Dr. Eleanor frequently references, create figure-eight patterns that harmonize all dimensions of your

being. These movements aren't just physical exercise—they're energetic integration.

5. **Recognize the spiritual nature of physical experience:**
Even seemingly mundane physical activities can become sacred when approached with presence and awareness. Eating, walking, breathing, and touching can be pathways to spiritual connection.

*Remember that your physical body exists in constant communion with all other dimensions of your being. When you honor this connection, your body becomes a vehicle for moving through the world and a temple for expressing your divine nature.*

CHAPTER 5

# THE SPIRITUAL/ARCHETYPAL - YOUR DIVINE ESSENCE

> *"The Spiritual/Archetypal World is the unifying, integrative field of consciousness. It is the world of REM sleep. Not deep sleep, but REM sleep, because it's the world where the Holy Spirit gives us messages that are only accessible in a slightly altered state of consciousness. A 'now you have it, now you don't' kind of consciousness."*

At the heart of your being exists a dimension that transcends the limitations of your Mental/Waking World constructs, emotional patterns, and physical form—the Spiritual/Archetypal. Spiritual living is not a distant realm accessible only to mystics and saints—it is the core of who you are, the essence from which all other dimensions of your being emerge.

The Spiritual/Archetypal is what Dr. Eleanor calls "the unified, integrated field of consciousness." It exists beyond judgment, beyond fear, beyond separation. It's the dimension where you know because you know because you know, and nobody can tell you that you don't know it.

Unlike the Mental/Waking World with its emphasis on thinking, the Emotional/Angelic World with its experiences of feeling, or the Physical/Biological World with its sensations, the Spiritual/Archetypal operates through direct knowing, intuitive wisdom, and connection to the divine flow of life.

Interestingly, Dr. Eleanor's research revealed that the Spiritual/Archetypal operates through a unique energetic matrix different from the other worlds. In this matrix, there is no ego center, no emotional center, and no cognitive center. It's a pure field of receptivity and being. The

Spiritual/Archetypal cannot be accessed primarily through thinking, feeling, or sensing—it requires a different mode of awareness.

## Characteristics of Spiritual/Archetypal Connection

The Spiritual/Archetypal communicates through whispers rather than shouts. Its voice is gentle, subtle, and requires attunement to hear. This whisper can easily be drowned out when you hear mental chatter that activates emotional reactivity or physical discomfort. To help with outside frequencies that are dissonant with your inner calm, use practices—essential for spiritual connection—that quiet your mind, calm your emotions, and relax your body's states of consciousness.

Even though the Spiritual/Archetypal frequency is subtle, it is also the most powerful dimension of being. From this dimension flows the energy, insight, and love that transform all other aspects of your experience. When you access your spiritual essence, you tap into unlimited resources of creativity, resilience, and wisdom.

## Strengthening Your Spiritual Connection

To enhance your connection to the Spiritual/Archetypal:

- **Create silent spaces in your life:**
  Meditation, contemplation, and time spent in nature create opportunities for spiritual awareness to emerge.

- **Listen for the whisper:**
  The voice of the spirit often comes as a gentle intuition, a quiet knowing, a subtle nudge. Practice attending to these whispers rather than waiting for thunderous revelations.

- **Use clean language with yourself:**
  When communicating with your spiritual nature, Dr. Eleanor recommends using "clean questions" that don't bias your

awareness in any direction. Questions like "What do I know now?" or "What would I like to have happen?" create space for authentic spiritual guidance to emerge.

- **Trust your knowing:**
When spiritual insight arises, honor it even if it doesn't make logical sense or align with what others believe. Your spiritual knowing is uniquely yours and doesn't require external validation.

- **Allow the Spiritual/Archetypal to transform the others:**
Remember, you can only alter emotional reactivity through spiritual awareness, mental constructs can only be elevated through a spiritual perspective, and physical experiences can only be fully honored through spiritual presence.

*As you develop your relationship with the Spiritual/Archetypal, you'll discover that it was never separate from the other dimensions of your life—it was always the essence flowing through them, waiting to be recognized, honored, and expressed.*

CHAPTER 6

# THE INTEGRATED WORLD - LIVING IN FLOW

*"When we integrate the energy of all Four Worlds, we can choose how we use the spiritual in all the worlds because the glue spiritually is love. And when love moves through you, and it activates the Mental/Waking World, the Spiritual/Archetypal, the Physical/Biological, and the Emotional/Angelic Worlds, we have an Integrated person, spiritually driven by the divine, but effectively manifesting in third-dimensional reality."*

The ultimate destination of your journey is not escape from any dimension of your being but the harmonious integration of all worlds into a coherent, flowing whole. This integration doesn't happen automatically—it requires conscious awareness, intention, and practice.

The Integrated World emerges when the Mental, Emotional, Physical, and Spiritual dimensions align. In this state, you think, feel, act, and perceive from the unified field of your whole being rather than from fragmented aspects of yourself.

Dr. Eleanor uses the figure eight symbol, also known as the infinity sign, to represent this integration. With this figure-eight movement, you physically trace the integration pathway between all worlds through practices like Tai Chi Gung. You move from Emotional to Mental to Physical to Spiritual and back again, creating a continuous flow where each dimension informs and enhances the others.

Integration doesn't mean that all dimensions are equally active at all times. Instead, you can fluidly access the appropriate dimension for each situation while remaining grounded in your spiritual essence. You might use Mental/Waking World skills to solve a practical problem,

Emotional/Angelic World awareness to process a challenging feeling, Physical/Biological World presence to enjoy sensory experience, and Spiritual/Archetypal wisdom to guide your overall direction—all while maintaining the thread of consciousness that connects these experiences.

## Signs of Integration

Signs that you're living in the Integrated World include:

- **Coherence:**
    - Your thoughts, feelings, actions, and intuitions align rather than contradict each other.
- **Flow:**
    - You move easily between different modes of being without getting stuck or fragmented.
- **Presence:**
    - You're fully available to each moment rather than caught in past regrets or future anxieties.
- **Authenticity:**
    - You express your true nature rather than conforming to external expectations or internal conditioning.
- **Resilience:**
    - You navigate challenges with flexibility and wisdom rather than rigid reactivity.

## To Cultivate Greater Integration:

- **Practice the figure eight:**
    - Through Tai Chi Gung or similar movement practices, physically trace the pattern of integration to embody this awareness.

- **Notice fragmentation:**
  - Become aware of when you operate from just one dimension and exclude others. Are you overthinking without feeling? Emotionally reacting without a spiritual perspective? Physically going through the motions without mental clarity?

- **Ask integrative questions:**
  - When making decisions or navigating challenges, consciously check in with all dimensions of your being. What does your mind understand? What does your heart feel? What does your body sense? What does your spirit know?

- **Release attachment to any single world:**
  - Each dimension has its own gifts and limitations. Integration comes from honoring all worlds rather than elevating one above the others.

- **Allow love to be the glue:**
  - As Dr. Eleanor notes, love is the force that binds all dimensions together. Cultivate love for yourself, others, and life as the foundation for integration.

*Living in the Integrated World doesn't mean you'll never face challenges or experience disharmony. Instead, it means you have the awareness and tools to recognize when you've fallen out of integration and the capacity to return to it. This is the dance of conscious living—continually returning to wholeness, moment by moment.*

# PART TWO:

## Foundation Practices

*These foundational practices create the groundwork for integrating all Four Worlds. They establish the basic skills and awareness necessary for more advanced applications.*

CHAPTER 7

# THE POWER OF BREATH AND MOVEMENT

"When you do the figure eight, if your right foot is in front, you will move Emotional/Angelic, Mental/Waking, Physical/Biological, Spiritual/Archetypal, and then back again. It's always tracing the dimensionality of the Four Worlds."

The transformation journey is not merely intellectual—you must embody the integration of the worlds through practices that integrate all dimensions of your being. Among the most powerful of these practices are conscious breathing and intentional movement.

Breath serves as a bridge between worlds. It operates automatically through your autonomic nervous system (Physical/Biological World), can be consciously controlled (Mental/Waking World), affects and is affected by emotions (Emotional/Angelic World), and connects you to life force energy (Spiritual/Archetypal). When you become conscious of your breath, you create an opportunity for integration across all dimensions.

## Transformational Breathing Patterns

Dr. Eleanor frequently recommends specific breathing patterns for transformation:

- **Balancing Breath:**
    - Inhale for a count of three, and exhale for a count of six to nine. The long exhale activates the parasympathetic nervous system, which reduces stress and creates space for spiritual awareness.

- **Releasing Breath:**
  - When experiencing emotional reactivity or stress, exhale fully while mentally releasing what no longer serves you. You might use the phrase from the Sedona Method: "Could I release it? Would I release it? When?"
- **Love and Peace Breath:**
  - Inhale while mentally saying "love," exhale while saying "peace." This simple practice realigns your energy field, creating coherence across all dimensions.

## The Figure-Eight Movement

Beyond breath, intentional movement creates powerful pathways for transformation. The figure-eight movement of Tai Chi Gung that Dr. Eleanor frequently references serves as a physical embodiment of the integration between all Four Worlds.

When performing this movement:

1. Start with awareness of your central column—the spine, or what Dr. Eleanor calls the "Satsuma," your essential self.
2. As you move in the figure-eight pattern, consciously trace the pathway between the Emotional, Mental, Physical, and Spiritual dimensions.
3. Allow stuck energy to release with each movement, creating space for new awareness to emerge.
4. Notice how the movement affects your energy field, thoughts, emotions, and spiritual connection.

## Other Integrative Movements

Other movement practices that support integration include walking in nature, swimming (which Dr. Eleanor particularly values for its immersive quality that blocks out external energies), and any form of dance or movement that brings you fully into present-moment awareness.

The key to transformative movement is not the specific form but the consciousness you bring to it. Any movement can become a spiritual practice when approached with intention, presence, and awareness of the interconnection between all dimensions of your being.

## Daily Practice Recommendation

*Practice moving with full consciousness daily, even for a few minutes. Notice how this practice gradually shifts your experience across all worlds, creating greater coherence, flow, and authentic expression.*

CHAPTER 8

# MEDITATION AND SACRED PRESENCE

> *"When you meditate and have your animals with you, it is easier to remain in that collective archetypal world you access when you sleep, and you can bring it to consciousness."*

Meditation is a direct pathway to the integrated field of consciousness, which Dr. Eleanor refers to as the Spiritual/Archetypal World. This practice creates space for the Mental/Waking World chatter to quiet, emotional reactivity to settle, and physical tension to release, allowing your spiritual essence to emerge into conscious awareness.

While countless meditation approaches exist, Dr. Eleanor particularly values Transcendental Meditation (TM) for its consistency and effectiveness. She notes that in her experience as a therapist, clients who practiced TM tended to maintain their practice more consistently than those using other methods. Within a week of beginning TM, Dr. Eleanor experienced tangible benefits regarding her physical stamina and mental clarity.

## Guidelines for Effective Meditation

Whatever meditation approach you choose, the key is consistency. Dr. Eleanor recommends meditating twice daily—once in the morning to set the tone for your day and once in the afternoon or early evening to reset and integrate your experiences.

- Create boundary conditions: Establish a regular time and place for meditation to signal to both your conscious and unconscious mind that this is a sacred space.

- Include your animals: Unlike some traditions that recommend meditating away from pets, Dr. Eleanor suggests including your animals in your meditation space. Because animals naturally exist in a different energetic matrix than humans—one without the mental, emotional, and ego centers that often dominate human consciousness—they can facilitate deeper spiritual connections.

- Transcend rather than concentrate: While some meditation approaches emphasize concentration or analysis, the most transformative approaches allow you to transcend mental activity altogether, accessing the field of pure awareness beyond thought.

- Allow rather than force: Effective meditation isn't about forcing your mind to be quiet but creating conditions where quietness naturally emerges. When thoughts arise, notice them without attachment and gently return to your meditation focus.

- Extend benefits beyond formal practice: The ultimate goal isn't just to experience peace or clarity during meditation and bring this awareness into all aspects of your life. Notice how regular meditation gradually shifts your experience in daily activities.

## Contemplative Practices

Beyond formal meditation, Dr. Eleanor values contemplative practices that integrate spiritual awareness into everyday experience. These might include:

- Walking in nature with a full presence
- Creating art or music as a spiritual expression
- Engaging in sacred movements like Tai Chi Gung
- Periods of silence and receptivity throughout your day
- Moments of conscious breathing between activities

## The Experience of Deep Meditation

The essence of meditation isn't about achieving any particular state but remembering your true nature. As you deepen your practice, you'll discover that meditation isn't something you do—it's something you become. The quietude, presence, and conscious awareness gradually permeate all aspects of your life, transforming how you perceive, respond, and engage with the world around you.

Dr. Eleanor reminds us that "when the divine breathes you, it's as though you're not breathing. The breath seems to permeate through the boundaries of your body." This experience of being "breathed by the divine" represents the ultimate integration, where the boundary between individual and universal consciousness dissolves into seamless oneness.

*In this sacred space of presence, the veil between worlds thins. You may experience what Dr. Eleanor describes as "knowing because you know because you know, and nobody can tell you that you don't know." This direct knowing transcends mental reasoning, emotional reaction, and physical sensation—it emerges from the unified field of your complete being and carries the unmistakable resonance of truth.*

CHAPTER 9

# DREAM CONSCIOUSNESS - MESSAGES FROM BEYOND

*"When you sleep, you function in a different matrix than when you're vertical. And when you sleep, you lose your mind. We lose the ego; we lose the emotions. We function, especially in deep sleep, about as close to comatose as we can be and still be alive and healthy."*

The realm of dreams offers a unique window into dimensions of consciousness that often remain inaccessible during waking hours. Dr. Eleanor's research revealed fascinating insights about the relationship between sleep, dreams, and our multidimensional nature.

When we sleep, we enter what Dr. Eleanor calls a different "matrix" or energy configuration. In deep sleep, we lose access to the mind (Crown and Ajna centers), the ego (Heart center), and emotional reactivity (Solar Plexus). We enter a realm of pure being, connected to the collective unconscious and archetypal energies that transcend individual identity.

## The Bridge of REM Sleep

During REM sleep, when dreaming occurs, something remarkable happens—energy from this pure spiritual dimension crosses over into your conscious awareness. Bringing between dimensions or worlds allows spiritual insight to flow into waking consciousness.

However, because consciousness is "state-specific," you can never fully capture the complete dream experience in your waking awareness. Dreams often feel fragmentary, symbolic, or elusive when you attempt to remember them upon waking. You're trying to translate experiences from one state of consciousness into another that operates by different rules.

## Working with Dream Consciousness

Despite this limitation, dreams offer profound opportunities for spiritual growth and integration when approached with consciousness and intention.

Dr. Eleanor offers several practices for working with dream consciousness:

- Program your dreams: Before sleep, set a clear intention for what you wish to explore or understand through your dreams. Many traditions teach that dreams can be directed through conscious intention, allowing you to use sleep time for spiritual work and problem-solving.

- Record dreams immediately: Keep a journal by your bed and write down dream fragments as soon as you wake, even if they seem incomplete or nonsensical. The longer you wait, the more the dream content will fade from conscious memory.

- Dialogue with dream elements: Using active imagination or journaling, converse with people, objects, or situations from your dreams. Ask what messages they have for you and allow responses to emerge without mental editing.

- Rewrite troubling dreams: If a dream contains disturbing or frightening elements, consciously rewrite it with a more empowering narrative. Dr. Eleanor notes that in some Pacific cultures, people routinely "rewrite" their dreams as part of their morning practice, recognizing that dreams exist as an alternate reality that can be shaped by intention.

- Listen for spiritual guidance: Dreams often contain messages, insights, or advice that your conscious mind might resist or dismiss during waking hours. Approach dream content with openness and curiosity rather than rigid interpretation.

- Notice collective patterns: Because dreams connect you to the collective unconscious, they may sometimes reflect collective energies or concerns beyond your personal experience. Such dreams occur more frequently during times of collective transition or crisis.

- Honor the animals: Dr. Eleanor notes that animals naturally exist in a consciousness matrix similar to what humans experience during sleep. Thus, many people feel such a profound connection with their animal companions—they serve as bridges to this deeper dimension of awareness.

## Integration Through Dream Work

Developing a conscious relationship with your dream life creates greater integration between your waking and sleeping consciousness. This integration allows spiritual awareness to flow more freely into all aspects of your experience, dissolving the artificial boundary between "spiritual" time and "ordinary" time.

*Remember that your spiritual nature doesn't disappear when you open your eyes in the morning—it simply shifts how it expresses through the different dimensions of your being. Dreamwork helps you recognize and honor the continuous presence of spirit throughout all states of consciousness.*

# PART THREE:

## Integration Practices

*These practices help you integrate the awareness and foundation skills from Parts One and Two into your daily life experience.*

CHAPTER 10

# JOURNALING FOR TRANSFORMATION

*"It's imperative to keep journals and write things down from the unconscious because you're bringing in the kinesthetic and the visual. And you're probably hearing the words as you write them. You're engaging your whole being and can help manifest and transform what you're dealing with."*

Journaling is one of the most powerful tools for integrating all dimensions of your being. When you write, you engage the Mental/Waking World through articulation, the Emotional/Angelic World through expression, the Physical/Biological World through the kinesthetic act of writing, and the Spiritual/Archetypal through accessing more profound wisdom.

Dr. Eleanor emphasizes handwritten journaling because it offers unique benefits compared to typing on a computer. Writing by hand activates different neural pathways, creating a more direct connection to your unconscious mind. Dr. Eleanor recommend keeping separate journals for various purposes, each dedicated to a specific aspect of your journey.

## Transformational Journaling Approaches

- Active Imagination: This technique, developed by Carl Jung, allows your unconscious to write through you without censorship or direction. Begin with a prompt or question, then write whatever emerges without judging or analyzing. This kind of writing creates a bridge between your conscious and unconscious awareness.

- Dialogue Journaling: This approach involves writing conversations between different aspects of yourself or between yourself and archetypes, guides, or even people from your life. For example, you might dialogue with a challenging emotion, asking:

Living from Soul | 47

- o "What do you want to have recognized?"
- o "What would you like me to know?"

Then, allow the "response" to emerge without mental interference.

- Paths Taken and Not Taken: Dr. Eleanor particularly value this journaling exercise, where you explore significant life-choice points. Consider moments when you made important decisions and reflect on your chosen path and the alternatives. This process creates a perspective on your life's journey and often reveals patterns and a sense of purpose.

- Clean Questions Journaling: Use clean questions as prompts for deeper exploration. Questions like "What do I know now?" or "What difference does this make?" create openings for authentic insight beyond mental construct.

- Four Worlds Journaling: Create separate sections or use different colored pens to explore experiences across all four dimensions of your being. How does a particular situation affect you mentally, emotionally, physically, and spiritually? What insights emerge when you integrate these perspectives?

- Gratitude Journaling: As discussed in Chapter 12, recording specific Gratitude with "because statements" creates powerful shifts in your awareness and experience across all dimensions.

## Maximizing Your Journaling Practice

For maximum benefit from your journaling practice:

- Create sacred space: Designate a specific time and place for journaling where you won't be interrupted. Treat this as necessary soul time rather than just another task.

- Release judgment: Allow whatever emerges to flow without criticism or censorship. The most valuable insights often come when you bypass the judging mind.

- Engage fully: Bring your complete presence to the practice rather than writing mechanically or distractedly. Feel the pen on the paper, notice your breath, and be aware of the emotions arising.

- Review periodically: Occasionally review past journal entries to notice patterns, growth, and insights that might not have been fully apparent in the moment.

- Honor what emerges: When significant insights arise through journaling, find ways to honor them through action, ritual, or further exploration rather than simply moving on to the next entry.

*Through consistent journaling practice, you create a tangible record of your inner journey and a powerful tool for integration across all dimensions of your being. If approached with sincere intention, this practice alone can catalyze profound transformation in your life.*

## CHAPTER 11

# CLEAN QUESTIONS AND AUTHENTIC COMMUNICATION

*"Clean language has no kinesthetic, auditory, or visual cues. And that's why I often say to you, What would you like to have happen? What do you know about this now? And when you know x, what difference does it make?"*

In your journey toward authentic living, how you communicate—both with yourself and others—plays a crucial role. However, most of our communication patterns were formed through socialization, conditioning, and mental constructs rather than emerging from deeper wisdom.

The powerful concept of "clean language" offers a way to access deeper dimensions of knowing. Clean language avoids all kinesthetic, auditory, and visual suggestions generally embedded in Mental/Waking World language. Because no perceptional bias exists in the question, the language allows you to deepen spiritual awareness and bridge worlds within your consciousness. I generally use "Clean Language" to deepen awareness.

Developed by David Grove, clean language uses questions that deliberately avoid directing or biasing the response. Unlike typical questions that often contain implicit assumptions or suggestions, clean questions create space for authentic insight to emerge.

## Why Clean Questions Work

Clean questions work because they bypass the Mental/Waking World's tendency to analyze, judge, and categorize. They create direct access to your intuitive knowing, emotional truth, physical wisdom, and spiritual insight.

Some examples of clean questions include:

1. "What would you like to have happen?"
2. "What do you know about this now?"
3. "Is there anything else about that?"
4. "What difference does that make?"
5. "And when that, what happens next?"

## Three Applications of Clean Questions

Use Clean Questions in three powerful ways:

**Transforming Reactivity**

Clean questions are particularly powerful for transforming emotional reactivity. When someone is upset or reactive, asking, "What would you like to have happen?" immediately shifts them from reactivity to consideration of the desired outcome. This question often "stops them dead in their tracks" and opens the door to more constructive engagement.

## Practicing Clean Communication

To practice clean communication:

1. Notice leading questions: Become aware of how often your questions (to yourself or others) contain assumptions, judgments, or directional cues.

2. Experiment with clean alternatives: Replace leading questions with clean versions and notice how this changes the quality of the response you receive.

3. Create space for authentic emergence: After asking a clean question, practice patience and deep listening. The most powerful insights often emerge from silence rather than immediate response.

4. Apply different approaches to different worlds: Recognize that various dimensions of experience may require different communication approaches. The Mental/Waking World might benefit from clarity and precision, the Emotional/Angelic World from mirroring and validation, the Physical/Biological World from sensory awareness, and the Spiritual/Archetypal World from clean questions that allow direct Inner Knowing to emerge.

*As you develop clear communication practices, you'll likely discover greater access to your wisdom and a more authentic connection with others. With world-appropriate communication, you create a foundation for Living from the Soul rather than from conditioning, reactivity, or limitation.*

CHAPTER 12

# GRATITUDE AS TRANSFORMATION

*"In people who've had medical procedures, if they start writing down their gratitude statements on the five days following the procedure, they heal better and faster than people who don't."*

*Gratitude is one of the most powerful catalysts for transformation across all dimensions of your being. Far from a simple mental exercise, authentic gratitude creates measurable shifts in your physical health, emotional state, mental clarity, and spiritual connection.*

*Research has confirmed what spiritual traditions have long taught: gratitude practice changes us. Studies show that people who engage in gratitude journaling experience "increased life satisfaction, decreased negative emotions, so there's a decrease in depression and an increase in feelings of self-fulfillment and self-esteem goes up. Sleep quality improves; relationship satisfaction and better communication happen."*

## Why Gratitude Transforms

What makes gratitude so transformative is that it directly counters the negativity bias of the human mind. Humans are neurologically wired to notice what's wrong, what's threatening, and what's missing. This survival mechanism served our ancestors well, but often leaves us stuck in fear, lack, and limitation. Gratitude deliberately redirects our attention to what's working, what's abundant, and what's supporting us.

## Dr. Eleanor's Gratitude Practice

I recommend a specific approach to gratitude practice that enhances its transformative power:

- Structure your gratitude across all Four Worlds: Identify specific things you're grateful for in each dimension—Mental, Emotional, Physical, and Spiritual. Including all four worlds ensures balanced awareness across your entire being.

- Add the "because statement": For each gratitude, add a specific reason that details the tangible, concrete effect on you. For example, rather than simply saying, "I'm grateful for my morning walk," you might say, "I'm grateful for my morning walk because it energizes my body, clears my mind, and connects me to the beauty of nature."

- Feel the gratitude physically: As you write or speak your gratitude, pause to feel the sensation of appreciation in your body. This anchors the practice in embodied experience, extending beyond mental concepts.

- Please make gratitude a daily practice: Consistency is key with gratitude. I practiced gratitude journaling daily for three years and found it profoundly shifted my awareness and values.

- Notice resistance: If you resist feeling grateful for certain aspects of your life, explore this with curiosity rather than judgment. Resistance often indicates areas where healing and transformation are needed.

## Gratitude During Challenges

Gratitude isn't about denying challenges or difficulties. Instead, it's about expanding your awareness to include the full spectrum of your experiences.

Even in circumstances that seem primarily negative, you can train yourself to notice what's supporting, teaching, and helping you grow.

For example, during illness, you might find gratitude for:

- The body's wisdom in demanding rest
- Healthcare providers offering support
- Friends and family expressing caring
- The opportunity to slow down and reflect
- Medications or treatments that provide relief
- What you can learn from the illness

Gratitude doesn't minimize the difficulty but places it within a larger context of support and meaning.

## Integration Practice: Four Worlds Gratitude

Each evening for the next week, identify one specific gratitude in each of the Four Worlds:

- Mental/Waking World: Something you learned, understood, or accomplished
- Emotional/Angelic World: A feeling you experienced or an emotional breakthrough that pushed you to think creatively
- Physical/Biological World: Something your body did well or a physical pleasure you enjoyed
- Spiritual/Archetypal World: A moment of connection, meaning, or inner knowing

Add the "because statement" to each gratitude statement, describing the specific impact or benefit you received.

*As you develop your gratitude practice, you'll likely notice that it becomes not just something you do but a lens through which you perceive life. This shift in perception gradually transforms every dimension of your being, creating greater harmony, joy, and authentic expression.*

# PART FOUR:

## Living Your Truth

*This section applies the understanding and practices from previous sections to real-world situations and life choices.*

## CHAPTER 13

# MANIFESTING FROM YOUR SOUL

> *"All of these experiences, the ones that bring you joy, the ones you love doing, the things that are strengths, all of those are about mobilizing your internal state, aligning with the divine energy, and then manifesting your dreams and living your purpose."*

The true art of manifestation emerges not from mental willpower or emotional wanting but from alignment with your soul's authentic expression. When you understand the multidimensional nature of manifestation, you move beyond simplistic "law of attraction" approaches into a more nuanced relationship with your creative energy.

Dr. Eleanor's research revealed that the manifestation process naturally takes approximately three months from inception to full expression in physical reality. This timeline isn't arbitrary but reflects the developmental pattern encoded in your energy field from before your birth. Just as a baby requires three months after birth to develop volition and choice, manifestations require this gestation period to form fully.

## The Elements of Authentic Manifestation

Understanding liberates you from the pressure of immediate results while offering a framework for conscious creation that honors all dimensions of your being. Authentic manifestation involves several key elements:

1. **Soul Alignment:** True manifestation begins with alignment to your spiritual essence rather than mental desires. Ask yourself, "Does this desire emerge from my authentic nature, conditioning, comparison, or compensation?" When your desires align with your soul's purpose, manifestation flows naturally rather than requiring force.

2. **Timing and Patience:** Honor the natural gestation period of manifestation rather than demanding immediate results. Dr. Eleanor recommends setting an intention and then allowing a week to pass before taking concrete action. If the intention still resonates after this period, proceed confidently while remaining open to refinement during the three-month manifestation cycle.

3. **Visualization with Feeling:** When visualizing desired outcomes, engage all senses, particularly the feeling state you wish to experience. Dr. Eleanor suggests recalling past experiences where you felt similarly empowered, successful, or fulfilled and using these as reference points for your manifestation. If an experience did not fulfill you, or if an experience was hurtful, consider your experience when responding in the present or when relating to another person.

4. **Specificity with Openness:** Be specific enough about your desired outcome to create clear direction, but open enough to allow divine intelligence to manifest in ways that might exceed your limited imagination. As Dr. Eleanor notes, "You do not want to be overly specific because you want to receive guidance from the Divine, your inner voice of knowing. And if you're too specific, it can't necessarily happen the way you visualized it."

5. **Release and Trust:** Once you've set your intention and taken appropriate action, release attachment to specific outcomes. Dr. Eleanor shares her approach to manifesting parking spaces: "All I do when I leave my house is I trust that I'm going to get a parking spot exactly where I'm going, and I never start to look before I arrive at my destination because if I did, I would be second-guessing the program."

6. **Integration Across All Worlds:** Effective manifestation engages all dimensions of your being—the clarity of the Mental/Waking

World, the passion of the Emotional/Angelic World, the embodied action of the Physical/Biological World, and the wisdom of the Spiritual/Archetypal World. When these align, manifestation becomes not a struggle but a natural expression of your integrated being.

## The True Purpose of Manifestation

One of Dr. Eleanor's most profound insights is that manifestation isn't primarily about getting things done but becoming more fully yourself. The external manifestations simply reflect and support your inner alignment and authentic expression. As she reminds us, "You're not doing it. You're allowing the divine to work through you."

This approach to manifestation honors both your divine nature and your human experience. You're neither a passive recipient of circumstance nor an all-powerful reality controller. Instead, you're a conscious co-creator, working with divine intelligence to express your unique gifts and fulfill your soul's purpose.

## Practical Manifestation Process

1. Connect with your spiritual essence through meditation or quiet reflection
2. Identify what wants to emerge from your soul rather than your ego
3. Visualize the desired outcome with all senses engaged
4. Feel the internal state you'll experience when manifestation occurs
5. Take inspired action when guidance emerges
6. Trust the process and remain open to unexpected forms
7. Express gratitude for what's already manifesting

*Remember that you manifest not to prove your power but to express your purpose. When manifestation serves your spiritual evolution and authentic contribution, it flows gracefully and effortlessly.*

CHAPTER 14

# NAVIGATING RELATIONSHIPS AUTHENTICALLY

*"When two people share the same values and are connected soul-wise, they monitor each other. They build each other's self-esteem. They don't tear it down."*

Relationships offer some of your most significant opportunities for growth, joy, and authentic expression—and also some of your most important challenges. Dr. Eleanor provides profound insights for navigating relationships from the soul rather than from conditioning, reaction, or limitation.

The foundation of authentic relationships begins with the understanding that relationships exist simultaneously across all Four Worlds. We connect mentally through shared ideas and communication, emotionally through feelings and responses, physically through proximity and touch, and spiritually through soul recognition and shared values.

## Problems in Fragmented Relationships

Relationship problems often emerge when a connection exists primarily in one or two worlds while missing in the others. For example, a relationship might have strong physical and emotional components but lack mental alignment or spiritual connection. True fulfillment comes from a relationship that honors and integrates all dimensions of being.

# Principles of Soul-Centered Relationships

Dr. Eleanor emphasizes several key principles for soul-centered relationships:

1. Value Alignment: Shared values are the most essential foundation for deep relationships. When two people align on fundamental values—what matters most, what constitutes integrity, what purpose serves—they create a strong foundation for navigating differences in other areas.

2. Mutual Monitoring: In healthy relationships, partners serve as mirrors and guides for each other's authentic expression. As Dr. Eleanor describes from her own 47+ year marriage: "When one of us veers off the path of our values, the other person brings them back." This mutual monitoring comes not from criticism but from love and commitment to each other's highest expression.

3. Appropriate Communication: Different relationship challenges require different communication approaches. Dr. Eleanor emphasizes the importance of identifying "who owns the problem" in any disagreement and using appropriate communication skills. Communication might involve active listening, clean questions, "I" statements about tangible effects, or simply providing space.

4. Transparency and Truth: An authentic relationship requires the courage to be transparent about your truth, even when it's uncomfortable. Dr. Eleanor shares her experience: "Transparency in relationships is beautiful." When you hide aspects of yourself or your experience, you create barriers to genuine connection.

5. Honoring Differences: Rather than expecting partners to be identical in perspective or expression, an authentic relationship honors the unique nature of each individual, including recognizing and respecting differences in how you process information, make decisions, express emotions, and connect spiritually.

## Navigating Relationship Challenges

When relationship challenges arise, Dr. Eleanor offers a simple framework for navigating them:

*"There are only three options that you have in any situation.*

- You can change yourself.
- You can change the other person.
- You change your environment."

Recognizing these limited options brings clarity to the decision-making process. If changing yourself would require compromising your integrity or authentic nature, and if the other person is unwilling or unable to change in ways that create greater alignment, then changing the environment (which might mean ending or significantly restructuring the relationship) may be necessary.

## Protecting Your Spiritual Nature

Dr. Eleanor emphasizes the importance of not compromising your spiritual nature for the sake of a relationship: "If you are hurt and you become emotionally reactive, then you're in a mental, Emotional/Angelic World. Once you transform in the Emotional/Angelic World, reactivity becomes a part of the spiritual dimension, and it's like a moving wave."

The highest expression of a relationship emerges when two people connect as whole beings, honoring all dimensions of themselves and each other. This mutual respect creates not dependency or limitation but mutual empowerment—a partnership of souls expressing their unique gifts while supporting each other's highest potential.

# Relationship Assessment Questions

To evaluate the health of your relationships across all Four Worlds, consider the following:

- The Mental/Waking World: Do you communicate clearly and respect each other's perspectives?
- Emotional/Angelic World: Do we support each other's emotional authenticity and growth?
- Physical/Biological World: Do we honor each other's physical needs and boundaries?
- Spiritual/Archetypal: Do we share fundamental values and support each other's spiritual evolution?

*When relationships align across all worlds, they become vehicles for mutual awakening and authentic expression.*

## CHAPTER 15

# SELF-CARE AS SPIRITUAL PRACTICE

*"When you take care of yourself properly, and you empower the inner Holy Spirit of the Self, that is the anchor, the 'I,' who you are, who you refer to, when you take care of that being, that comes first. Because without caring for yourself, you cannot properly care for anyone else."*

Dr. Eleanor offers a radically different perspective in a culture that often glorifies self-sacrifice and busyness: self-care isn't selfish but essential to authentic living. Far from a luxury or indulgence, proper self-care forms the foundation for expressing your spiritual nature in all aspects of life.

Self-care extends far beyond occasional pampering or relaxation. It encompasses how you nourish, rest, move, and honor your body; engage, challenge, and quiet your mind; process, express, and transform your emotions; and connect with, listen to, and live from your spiritual essence.

## Four Worlds Self-Care

Dr. Eleanor emphasizes that effective self-care requires awareness of all Four Worlds and the unique needs of each:

1. Physical/Biological World Self-Care: Honor your body's needs for appropriate nourishment, movement, rest, touch, and environmental support. Notice how often these basic needs get sacrificed to mental priorities or emotional patterns. Dr. Eleanor emphasizes listening to your body's wisdom rather than overriding it with mental directives.

2. Mental/Waking World Self-Care: Create boundaries around information intake, screen time, and mental stimulation. Practice

discernment about what thoughts you entertain and what perspectives you adopt—schedule time for intellectual engagement and mental quietude. Notice how mental clutter or constant input can deplete your energy and cloud your clarity.

3. Emotional/Angelic World Self-Care: Develop healthy ways to acknowledge, express, and process emotions rather than suppressing or being controlled by them. Create relationships and environments that support emotional authenticity and transformation. Recognize that emotional energy needs a spiritual perspective to transform rather than simply recycling.

4. Spiritual/Archetypal Self-Care: Prioritize practices that connect you to your spiritual essence—meditation, prayer, time in nature, creative expression, and service to others. Create regular opportunities to quiet the mental chatter and emotional reactivity that can drown out the whisper of spirit. Honor what your soul needs to thrive rather than what your conditioning or others' expectations demand.

## The Discipline of Self-Care

Self-care requires both awareness and discipline. Dr. Eleanor emphasizes the importance of structure and commitment: "We must work on all levels. It's not enough to practice Tai Chi Gung (or another spiritual practice) and hope everything clears. You must do the inner work and spiritual practices so your consciousness remains constant while meditating and practicing, and you must remain disciplined. Self-care takes energy, and it takes commitment."

She suggests creating a detailed inventory of your self-care needs across all Four Worlds, noticing where you currently prioritize care and where you might neglect essential aspects of your well-being. This inventory becomes not a rigid schedule but a conscious recognition of what truly sustains you.

## Transforming Self-Relationship

Perhaps most importantly, self-care requires shifting how you speak to yourself. Dr. Eleanor encourages "treating yourself like you would treat your most cherished loved one" and "giving yourself the advice you would give your most cherished loved one." This shift in self-relationship transforms self-care from an obligation into an expression of self-love.

Committing to comprehensive self-care creates a foundation for authentic living that ripples outward into all your relationships and activities. Far from making you self-centered, proper self-care enables you to be more genuinely present and give to others because you're operating from a state of fullness rather than depletion.

## Self-Care Assessment

Complete this inventory across all Four Worlds:

- Physical/Biological: What does my body need for optimal health and vitality?
- Mental/Waking: What supports my mental clarity and peace?
- Emotional/Angelic: What helps me process and transform emotions healthily?
- Spiritual/Archetypal: What connects me to my deeper purpose and essence?

Notice which areas receive adequate attention and which you neglect. Begin with small, consistent changes rather than overwhelming yourself with dramatic shifts.

*Dr. Eleanor reminds us, "If you're not honoring yourself as much as you honor any other person you make an appointment with, you're cheating yourself." When you truly honor all dimensions of your being, you create the conditions for your spiritual essence to flow freely through every aspect of your life.*

CHAPTER 16

# DISCOVERING YOUR LIFE PURPOSE

*"One of the keys to managing your life is to ask who in your life lives the way they claim to be living. And if someone is pretending to live one way and is actually saying something different or doing something different, that's very telling."*

Every life contains a pattern—a series of stepping stones that, when viewed with awareness, reveal your soul's unique path and purpose. These stepping stones aren't always the dramatic moments or obvious achievements, but often include seemingly minor choices, encounters, and experiences that subtly shift your direction.

Dr. Eleanor emphasizes the value of conscious reflection on your life path, particularly through exploring "paths taken and not taken." When you examine key decision points in your life and consider your choices and the alternatives not chosen, you often discover the invisible thread of purpose running through your journey.

## Approaches to Uncovering Purpose

To uncover your life purpose, Dr. Eleanor suggests several approaches:

1. Childhood Joy: Return to what brought you joy and absorption as a child before external expectations and conditioning shaped your choices. What activities made you lose track of time? What naturally attracted your interest and attention? These early attractions often contain seeds of your authentic purpose.

2. Strengths and Gifts: Identify activities and contributions that come naturally to you, where you excel without excessive effort.

Dr. Eleanor notes that purpose often lies at the intersection of your natural gifts and service to others.

3. Meaningful Challenges: Look at difficulties you've faced not as random obstacles but as specific growth opportunities for your soul. What qualities have you developed through challenges? What insights have you gained? How might these prepare you for your unique contribution?

4. Synchronicities: Notice patterns of "meaningful coincidence" in your life—events that seem to align perfectly despite statistical improbability. These synchronicities often point toward your soul's direction and provide confirmation when you align with your purpose.

5. Inner Knowing: Ultimately, your purpose reveals itself through inner knowing rather than external validation. As Dr. Eleanor emphasizes, "When the Holy Spirit speaks to you and gives you a task, you don't have a lot of choice if you want to be conscious."

## Purpose Across the Four Worlds

Finding and living your purpose isn't about discovering one specific career or activity but aligning all dimensions of your being with your authentic essence. Purpose manifests differently across the Four Worlds:

- In the Mental/Waking World, purpose appears as clarity, focus, and meaningful contribution.
- In the Emotional/Angelic World, purpose feels like passion, fulfillment, and resonance.
- In the Physical/Biological World, purpose gives you an energetic flow, vitality, and embodied presence.
- In the Spiritual/Archetypal World, purpose emanates as alignment, integrity, and divine connection.

# Following Your Joy

Dr. Eleanor emphasizes the importance of doing what you love: "I've never worked a day in my life because I've only done what I love." Loving what you do does not mean avoiding all challenging or demanding tasks; rather, it is about ensuring that your primary activities align with what feeds your soul.

When you discover activities that bring you joy, Dr. Eleanor recommends asking:

- What about this experience resonates with me?
- What qualities or energies does this experience evoke?
- How might I bring more of this essence into my life?"

This inquiry helps you identify the underlying qualities of your purpose rather than limiting it to specific forms or contexts.

# The Courage to Live Purpose

Living your purpose requires courage—the willingness to follow your inner guidance even when it contradicts conventional expectations or established patterns. Dr. Eleanor shares her own experience: "Follow your dream. If you don't follow your dream, you will regret that you didn't."

As you align more fully with your authentic purpose, you'll likely notice greater synchronicity, flow, and support from seemingly random circumstances. However, being aligned does not mean the absence of challenges but rather a sense that even difficulties somehow serve your deeper growth and contribution. When you align with your soul's intention, you trust your capacities and the larger intelligence that works through you.

## Purpose Discovery Exercise

Reflect on these questions in your journal:

- What activities made you lose track of time as a child?
- What comes easily to you that others find difficult?
- What challenges have shaped your character and wisdom?
- What synchronicities have pointed you in specific directions?
- When do you feel most alive and authentic?
- What contribution would you regret not making?

*Notice patterns and themes that emerge across your responses. Your purpose often lies at the intersection of your natural gifts, life experiences, and the world's needs.*

# PART FIVE:

## Advanced Applications

*These final chapters address the deeper challenges and opportunities of living authentically in complex circumstances.*

CHAPTER 17

# NAVIGATING FEAR AND TRANSFORMATION

*"One of the things that is on my mind to talk about is fear. Because all of you are evolving in consciousness, as you move out of 3D into 4D, 5D, and above, you are always in danger of losing your grounding and expanding big."*

The journey of spiritual growth inevitably brings encounters with fear. As you expand beyond familiar boundaries and conditioned patterns, the ego-self often experiences this expansion as threatening rather than liberating. Understanding and navigating fear with awareness becomes essential for continued growth and authentic expression.

## Types of Transformational Fear

Dr. Eleanor identifies several types of fear that commonly arise in the transformational journey:

1. Fear of the Unknown: As you move beyond familiar mental constructs and emotional patterns, you enter territory your culturally bound self cannot map or control. Being misaligned with your core Self creates fear, not because the unknown is threatening, but because you identify familiarity with safety.

2. Fear of Dissolution: Deep transformation often involves releasing aspects of identity that no longer serve your authentic expression. Releasing old patterns can trigger fear of "losing yourself" or disappearing. As Dr. Eleanor notes from one of her Kundalini experiences: "The fear was of death. Because at the moment of death, our memory is obliterated, and we are reborn."

3. Fear of Power: Paradoxically, many people fear their limitations and true power. Owning your authentic capacities brings responsibilities and visibility that the conditioned self may resist. As Marianne Williamson famously wrote, "Our deepest fear is not that we are inadequate. Our deepest fear is that we are powerful beyond measure."

4. Fear of Judgment: As you begin living more authentically, you may trigger discomfort or disapproval from others who remain invested in old patterns or expectations. This social resistance can activate deep fears of rejection or isolation.

5. Fear of Physical Symptoms: The transformational journey often creates temporary physical symptoms as energy shifts and blocked patterns get released. Without understanding, these manifestations can generate fear that something is wrong rather than recognition that something is transforming.

## Navigating Fear with Awareness

Dr. Eleanor emphasizes that these fears are normal aspects of growth rather than indications to retreat or contract. She offers several approaches for navigating fear with awareness:

1. Physical Grounding: Practices such as Tai Chi Gung, conscious walking, or simply feeling your feet on the earth help stabilize expanding awareness in your physical body. As Dr. Eleanor notes, "Doing your Tai Chi Gung, which keeps you in the body, is a protection."

2. Release Techniques: When fear arises, use simple techniques like the Sedona Method: "Could I release it? Would I release it? When?" These questions create space between your awareness and the fear rather than keeping you identified with it.

3. Purpose Questioning: Ask, "What is this fear teaching me? What growth or awareness is it inviting?" This shifts from resistance to curiosity and from victimhood to empowerment.

4. Compassionate Presence: Rather than judging fear as weakness or failure, bring a gentle awareness. Notice where you feel it in your body, what thoughts accompany it, and what emotions intertwine with it. This presence often allows fear to transform naturally.

5. Community Support: Connect with others who understand the transformational journey rather than attempting to navigate it in isolation. Dr. Eleanor notes, "If all of us who are Spiritual join together without fear, with a sense of trust in God, a trust in the divine coming through us, then we each become a beacon of light."

## Understanding Physical Symptoms

Physical symptoms accompanying spiritual awakening, such as sensations of heat, tingling, pressure, or unusual energy movements, often trigger particular concerns. Dr. Eleanor shares from her own Kundalini experiences that these manifestations, while sometimes uncomfortable, represent energy-clearing blockages that create new pathways in you. Rather than resisting these sensations, she suggests thanking them as evidence of transformation in progress.

## Fear as a Messenger

Perhaps most importantly, Dr. Eleanor emphasizes that transformation isn't about eliminating fear but about changing your relationship with it. Fear becomes not an enemy to vanquish but a messenger carrying information about where healing, integration, or expansion occurs.

As you navigate the transformational journey, remember that fear itself cannot harm you—only your response to fear determines whether it becomes limiting or liberating. When approached with awareness, even the most intense fear becomes another aspect of your experiences that you witness, honor, and integrate into your expanding consciousness.

CHAPTER 18

# LIVING AUTHENTICALLY IN A CHALLENGING WORLD

*"When you stay inside your spiritual self, clarifying your spiritual values and their integrity, and you don't compromise what you know is right for you, you're protected. When you align with your divinity, nothing touches you."*

The ultimate challenge isn't merely achieving spiritual awareness but embodying it amid the complexities, demands, and challenges of everyday life. Dr. Eleanor offers profound guidance for maintaining an authentic connection to your soul while navigating a world that often operates from very different values and awareness.

## Conscious Engagement Across the Four Worlds

Living authentically requires discernment about where and how to engage across the Four Worlds:

- Mental/Waking World Engagement: Recognize when interactions require Mental/Waking World skills like clear communication, boundary-setting, and practical problem-solving. Develop the capacity to engage at this level without being limited to it. As Dr. Eleanor advises: "When you are in the Mental/Waking World, be there consciously."

- Emotional/Angelic World Navigation: Learn to recognize emotional reactivity—in yourself and others—and develop skills for transforming rather than just expressing or suppressing these energies. Remember that emotional reactions always point to something deeper than their apparent triggers.

- Physical/Biological World Wisdom: Honor your body's messages rather than overriding them with mental directives or emotional patterns. Recognize how physical practices and environments either support or undermine your authentic expression.

- Spiritual/Archetypal Anchoring: Maintain a consistent connection to your spiritual essence through formal practices and moment-by-moment awareness. As Dr. Eleanor emphasizes, "If you're not staying in spiritual alignment, then your life won't work as well as it could."

## Navigating Challenging Relationships

Perhaps the greatest challenge of authentic living involves relationships with people who operate from different levels of consciousness or contradictory values. Dr. Eleanor offers several approaches for navigating these situations:

- Conscious Disengagement: When someone's energy or perspective requires you to compromise your integrity, practice what Dr. Eleanor calls "leaving the field." Disengagement isn't about judgment but about honoring your boundaries and truth.

- Appropriate Communication: Adjust your communication approach based on the other person's current state rather than expecting them to meet you at your level. Sometimes, this means simplifying, listening without advice, and asking clean questions that create openings for deeper awareness.

- Compassionate Perspective: Remember that unconscious behavior reflects limitation rather than malice. As Dr. Eleanor notes: "If they're not as conscious as you, they need all the love and kindness they can get."

- Strategic Transparency: Be discerning about where, when, and with whom you share your deepest truths. Your decisions about sharing your depth aren't about dishonesty, but rather recognizing that not everyone receives or respects certain aspects of your experience.

## Honoring Different Levels of Connection

Living authentically includes honoring the reality that different relationships will connect at various levels. Dr. Eleanor shares her experience: "I can't talk about spirituality in my family of origin. I have a sister who doesn't talk to me because she's an atheist, and I am committed to God." Rather than trying to force all relationships to engage at all levels, recognize where genuine connection is possible and where it isn't.

## Transforming Challenges into Growth

When challenging circumstances arise, Dr. Eleanor recommends asking:

- "What is so important that God would put this in front of me?
- And what is the lesson I need to learn?
- What do I need to know?"

This perspective transforms difficulties from random obstacles into specific growth opportunities aligned with your soul's evolution.

## The Source of True Protection

Perhaps most importantly, authentic living requires remembering that you are never alone in your journey. Beyond human companionship, you exist in constant communion with divine presence. As Dr. Eleanor reminds us: "The Holy Spirit is within each of us, and we are divine. Our self is divine. When we look only outside of ourselves for the divine, we miss the integrated self that is divine."

This inner communion provides the strength, clarity, and resilience to live from the soul, even when external circumstances seem to oppose or undermine this alignment. It allows you to maintain inner peace amid outer chaos, to express love in the face of fear, and to embody truth regardless of external validation or resistance.

## The Practice of Inner Sanctuary

As Dr. Eleanor summarizes: "If you stay inside yourself and be at peace... the key for all of us is becoming conscious and not being limited in our thinking or our imagination by the limitations falsely imposed upon us."

*When you anchor yourself in this inner sanctuary of your authentic being, you discover that external circumstances have far less power to disturb your essential peace than you once believed. Internal alignment doesn't mean you become passive or disconnected from the world, but engage from a place of centered strength rather than reactive vulnerability.*

CONCLUSION

# THE JOURNEY CONTINUES

> *"We're now functioning in a society that has lost its way from a sociological, anthropological, and psychological perspective. And it's a development on a cultural level that is unprecedented from what I know of all of my studying of cultures around the world."*

As we end this exploration, we recognize that Living From Soul isn't a destination but a continuous journey of awakening, integration, and authentic expression. The path doesn't end with understanding concepts or profound experiences—it involves the daily, moment-by-moment choice to live from your most profound truth and integrity rather than from a want for approval, control, reactivity, or limitation.

Dr. Eleanor reminds us that we live in extraordinary times—a period of profound transition where old structures, beliefs, and ways of being dissolve while new possibilities emerge. This transition creates unprecedented challenges and opportunities for those committed to conscious evolution.

## The Map and the Territory

The Four Worlds framework offers a map for this journey—a way to recognize where you're operating from at any moment and how to integrate all dimensions of your being into coherent wholeness. This integration doesn't happen automatically or immediately but unfolds through consistent practice, awareness, and intention.

The practices and perspectives suggested invite you to discover your authentic path. Your journey will contain elements unique to your soul's purpose and evolution—specific challenges, gifts, and expressions that differ from anyone else's. Honor this uniqueness rather than attempting to conform to external templates or expectations.

## Essential Truths for the Journey

As you continue your journey of Living from Soul, remember these essential truths:

- You are already whole: The journey isn't about becoming something you're not, but about remembering and expressing who you truly are beneath layers of living in the Mental/Waking World.

- Integration is your goal: Rather than escaping the Mental/Waking, Emotional/Angelic, or Physical/Biological Worlds for spiritual experiences, the Integrated path involves bringing Spiritual/Archetypal awareness into all dimensions of your being.

- Trust your knowing: **When you know because you know because you know,** honor this knowing even when it contradicts external voices or expectations.

- The Four Worlds need each other: Each dimension of your being offers essential gifts and perspectives. True wisdom emerges not from any single world but from their harmonious integration.

- You are not alone: You journey within a field of consciousness that contains and connects all beings. Your awakening contributes to collective evolution, just as collective evolution supports your journey.

## Beyond the Maps

In closing, I offer Dr. Eleanor's profound reminder: "You live in your soul; you don't live in your mind. So I don't care what your charts show. Your spiritual values guide you, so don't get hung up on the maps. They're a tool for understanding the Four Worlds, but they are not the end-all because it's still a work in progress from a scientific standpoint."

This book's maps, frameworks, and practices point you toward your own direct experience of wholeness and authentic living. Use them as guides, but never let them substitute for your inner knowing and spiritual connection.

## Your Unique Contribution

As you fully embody this work, you become what Dr. Eleanor calls "a beacon of light"—someone whose integrated presence naturally supports others in their awakening. Your transformational process isn't about teaching or preaching but simply about living authentically from your complete nature.

Your journey of living from soul ripples outward in ways you may never fully comprehend. Each moment of authentic choice, each return to integration, and each response from love rather than fear contributes to the collective healing and evolution our world desperately needs.

May your journey of living from soul bring ever-deepening joy, authentic expression, and conscious contribution to a world in profound need of awakened presence.

## APPENDIX A

# FOUR WORLDS SELF-ASSESSMENT

Use this assessment to clarify your current patterns across all dimensions of your being. Answer honestly without judgment—this is simply information to support your growth.

## Mental/Waking World Assessment

Rate each statement from 1 (never) to 5 (always):

- I think clearly without getting caught in mental loops
- I can focus on tasks without excessive distraction
- My internal dialogue is generally supportive and constructive
- I make decisions based on clear thinking rather than overthinking
- I can be present without getting lost in past or future concerns
- I communicate my thoughts clearly and effectively
- I question limiting beliefs rather than accepting them automatically
- I use my analytical abilities to serve my deeper purposes

Total Mental/Waking World Score: ___/40

## Emotional/Angelic World Assessment

Rate each statement from 1 (never) to 5 (always):

- I feel my emotions entirely without being overwhelmed by them
- I can transform emotional reactivity into a conscious response
- I express emotions appropriately rather than suppressing or exploding

- I use emotional experiences as opportunities for growth and wisdom
- I maintain emotional balance during challenging situations
- I feel compassion for myself and others during difficult emotions
- I can be present with others' emotions without taking them on
- I experience a full range of emotions as natural and valuable

Total Emotional/Angelic World Score: ___/40

## Physical/Biological World Assessment

Rate each statement from 1 (never) to 5 (always):

- I listen to my body's signals about rest, nutrition, and movement
- I maintain physical practices that support my overall well-being
- I feel comfortable and at home in my physical body
- I use physical sensation as guidance for decisions and choices
- I speak to my body with kindness and appreciation
- I honor my body's natural rhythms and needs
- I enjoy physical pleasures without guilt or excess
- I treat my body as a sacred temple rather than just a vehicle

Total Physical/Biological World Score: ___/40

## Spiritual/Archetypal Assessment

Rate each statement from 1 (never) to 5 (always):

- I maintain regular practices that connect me to my spiritual essence
- I trust my intuitive knowing even when it contradicts logic
- I feel connected to something greater than myself
- I make decisions based on spiritual values and inner guidance
- I experience life as meaningful and purposeful
- I maintain a spiritual connection during challenging times

- I feel love and compassion as my natural state
- I live from an authentic purpose rather than external expectations

Total Spiritual/Archetypal Score: ___/40

## Integration Assessment

Rate each statement from 1 (never) to 5 (always):

- My thoughts, feelings, actions, and intuitions generally align
- I can fluidly move between different modes of being as appropriate
- I remain present and centered during daily activities
- I express my authentic nature rather than conforming to expectations
- I navigate challenges with flexibility and wisdom
- I feel coherent and whole rather than fragmented
- I honor all aspects of my being equally
- I live from integrated awareness rather than single-world dominance

Total Integration Score: ___/40

## Interpreting Your Scores

- 35-40: Strong Integration - This world is well-developed and integrated into your life
- 25-34: Moderate Development- This area has a good foundation, but room for growth
- 15-24: Emerging Awareness - This world needs focused attention and development
- Below 15: Significant Growth Opportunity - This area requires priority attention

## Creating Your Development Plan

- Identify your strongest world - How can you use this strength to support development in other areas?
- Identify your development priorities - Which 1-2 worlds would benefit most from focused attention?
- Notice patterns - Are there specific themes across the worlds that suggest particular practices or areas of focus?
- Choose specific practices - Based on your assessment, which practices from this book feel most relevant and accessible?

APPENDIX B

# DAILY INTEGRATION PRACTICES

*These practices help you integrate Four Worlds awareness into your daily life. Choose 2-3 that resonate most strongly and commit to them for at least 30 days.*

## Morning Practices

Four Worlds Check-In (5 minutes) - Upon waking, before getting out of bed:

- Mental/Waking World: What is my mind's state right now?
- Emotional/Angelic World: What emotions are present?
- Physical/Biological World: How does my body feel?
- Spiritual/Angelic World: What does my soul need today?

Intention Setting (3 minutes) - Set a daily intention that honors all Four Worlds:

- How do I want to think today?
- How do I want to feel today?
- How do I want to care for my body today?
- How do I want to connect spiritually today?

Gratitude Practice (5 minutes) - Identify one specific gratitude in each world with a "because statement":

- Mental/Waking World: Something you learned or understood
- Emotional/Angelic World: A feeling you appreciated
- Physical/Biological World: Something your body did well
- Spiritual/Angelic World: A moment of connection or meaning

## Throughout the Day

Breath Awareness - Several times daily, take three conscious breaths:

- Breath 1: Notice your mental state
- Breath 2: Notice your emotional state
- Breath 3: Connect to your spiritual center

Clean Questions Check-In - When facing decisions or challenges, ask:

- What do I know about this now?
- What would I like to have happen?
- What difference would that make?

Body Wisdom Pause - Before important decisions, check with your body:

- How does Option A feel in my body?
- How does Option B feel in my body?
- What is my physical intuition telling me?

## Evening Practices

Four Worlds Review (10 minutes) - Reflect on your day across all dimensions:

- Mental/Waking World: How did I use my thinking today? What did I learn?
- Emotional/Angelic World: What emotions did I experience? How did I handle them?
- Physical/Biological World: How did I care for my body? What did it need?
- Spiritual/Angelic World: How did I connect to my deeper purpose? What guidance emerged?

Integration Journaling (10 minutes) - Write about:

- Where did I feel most integrated today?

- Where did I notice fragmentation?
- What would I do differently tomorrow?
- What am I grateful for in each world?

Release and Reset (5 minutes) - Before sleep:

- Consciously release the day's tensions and concerns
- Set an intention for restorative sleep
- Thank your body for its service
- Connect to your spiritual essence

## Weekly Practices

Paths Taken/Not Taken Reflection - Once weekly, reflect on a significant choice point in your life:

- What path did I take?
- What alternative paths were available?
- What have I learned from the path I chose?
- How has this choice contributed to my soul's evolution?

Four Worlds Assessment - Weekly check-in using the assessment tool in Appendix A:

- Which world felt most integrated this week?
- Which world needs more attention?
- What patterns am I noticing?
- What adjustments would support better integration?

Nature Connection - Spend at least 30 minutes in nature weekly with conscious Four Worlds awareness:

- Mental/Waking World: Notice thoughts arising and releasing
- Emotional/Angelic World: Feel your emotional response to natural beauty
- Physical/Biological World: Engage all your senses fully

- Spiritual/Angelic World: Connect to the larger intelligence of nature

## Monthly Practices

Deep Integration Review - Once a month, conduct a comprehensive review:

- How has my Four Worlds integration evolved?
- What practices are most effective for me?
- What challenges am I still navigating?
- What wants to emerge in the coming month?

Purpose Alignment Check - Monthly assessment of life direction:

- Are my daily activities aligned with my deeper purpose?
- Where am I living authentically vs. from expectations?
- What adjustments would bring greater alignment?
- How is my soul calling me to grow or serve?

## APPENDIX C

# TROUBLESHOOTING COMMON CHALLENGES

### "I can't quiet my mind during meditation."

Understanding: The Mental/Waking World's natural function is to think. The goal isn't to stop thoughts but to change your relationship with them and to expand your thinking into the Emotional/Angelic World of Creative Intelligence.

Solutions:

- Try transcendental approaches rather than concentration methods
- Use gentle awareness rather than forced quieting
- Remember that noticing thoughts IS awareness
- Consider guided meditations or mantra-based practices
- Start with shorter sessions (5-10 minutes)

### "I feel overwhelmed by emotions."

Understanding: The Emotional/Angelic World becomes overwhelming when it lacks a spiritual perspective for transformation.

Solutions:

- Practice the five-step emotional transformation process (Chapter 3)
- Use breathing techniques to create space around emotions
- Remember that emotions are energy in motion; they are meant to flow
- Seek support from others who understand emotional processing
- Consider that overwhelm often signals the need for better boundaries

## "I don't feel connected to my body."

Understanding: The Physical/Biological World functions beneath conscious awareness most of the time. We handle our physical/biological needs and insights in ways that may disconnect us from awareness, understanding, and wisdom.

Solutions:

- Start with simple body awareness practices (breathing, sensing)
- Engage in movement that feels pleasurable rather than obligatory
- Practice speaking kindly to your body
- Notice how different foods, activities, and environments affect your energy
- Consider bodywork, massage, or other healing touch practices

## "I can't access my spiritual connection."

Understanding: The Spiritual/Archetypal World communicates subtly and can be drowned out by noise from the other worlds.

Solutions:

- Create regular quiet time without external stimulation
- Spend time in nature
- Practice asking clean questions and listening for responses
- Notice what brings you joy, peace, or a sense of meaning
- Remember that spiritual connection is your natural state, not something to achieve

## "I feel fragmented and can't integrate."

Understanding: Integration is a practice, not a permanent state. Fragmentation often signals areas needing attention.

Solutions:

- Use the Four Worlds check-in practice throughout your day

- Notice which world tends to dominate and gently include the others
- Practice the figure-eight movement to embody integration
- Be patient—integration develops gradually through consistent practice
- Celebrate moments of integration rather than focusing on fragmentation

## "People don't understand my spiritual journey."

Understanding: Not everyone is at the same stage of consciousness development, and that's natural.

Solutions:

- Find community with others on similar paths
- Practice discernment about who to share deeply with
- Focus on living your truth rather than convincing others
- Remember that your authentic presence teaches more than words
- Maintain compassion for others' limitations while protecting your growth

## "I keep falling back into old patterns."

Understanding: Socialization in a culture runs deep, and transformation happens in spirals rather than straight lines.

Solutions:

- Celebrate awareness of old patterns—that's already progress
- Use relapses as information about what still needs healing
- Practice self-compassion rather than self-judgment
- Strengthen your spiritual practices during vulnerable times
- Remember that each return to consciousness is easier than the last

## "I feel guilty about prioritizing self-care."

Understanding: Children often learn that self-care is selfish but essential for authenticity and service.

Solutions:

- Recognize that you can't give what you don't have
- Reframe self-care as a spiritual practice and preparation for service
- Start with small, non-negotiable self-care practices
- Notice how better self-care improves your relationships and contributions
- Remember that modeling self-care teaches others to value themselves

## "I'm afraid of what others will think if I live authentically."

Understanding: Fear of judgment often keeps you trapped in inauthentic patterns that serve no one.

Solutions:

- Start with small, authentic choices in safe environments
- Remember that others' opinions reflect their limitations, not your truth
- Find support from people who celebrate your authenticity
- Practice connecting to your spiritual center when fear arises
- Focus on the regret you'll feel if you don't live authentically

## "I don't know what my purpose is."

Understanding: Purpose often emerges gradually through living authentically rather than being discovered through thinking.

Solutions:

- Follow what brings you joy and energy

- Notice what comes easily to you that others find difficult
- Pay attention to synchronicities and meaningful coincidences
- Explore the themes and patterns in your life story
- Trust that purpose reveals itself through authentic living

## "I feel like I'm not making progress."

Understanding: Spiritual growth often happens in ways that aren't immediately visible or measurable.

Solutions:

- Keep a journal to track subtle changes over time
- Notice improvements in how you handle familiar challenges
- Ask trusted friends if they've noticed changes in you
- Remember that consciousness shifts can be invisible but profound
- Focus on consistency in practice rather than dramatic results

# ABOUT DR. ELEANOR

Dr. Eleanor has devoted over five decades to exploring the multidimensional nature of human consciousness through her work as a clinical psychologist, researcher, and spiritual guide. Trained at the University of Chicago in the world's first interdisciplinary social science program, she brings together perspectives from psychology, biology, sociology, and anthropology, reflecting the Four Worlds framework she teaches.

Her approach emerged from rigorous academic research and profound personal experience, including multiple Kundalini awakenings that transformed her understanding of consciousness. She developed the Noble Energy Maps®, a system that provides a comprehensive framework for understanding the energetic patterns that shape human development and expression across all dimensions of being.

Throughout her career, Dr. Eleanor has maintained that authentic living requires integrating all aspects of our nature rather than elevating one dimension above others. Her work consistently emphasizes direct knowing over external authority, personal experience over abstract theory, and authentic expression over conformity to conditioning.

She often reminds her students: "I've never worked a day in my life because I love what I do, and I do what I love." This integration of purpose, passion, and service exemplifies the approach to Living From Soul that she has taught and embodied throughout her remarkable journey.

Her research, with over 45,000 cases, has created the only scientifically documented spiritual system, bridging the gap between empirical research and transformational practice. The Four Worlds framework and Noble Energy Maps® represent decades of careful observation, documentation, and refinement of understanding about human consciousness and authentic living.

Dr. Eleanor continues to guide individuals and groups in discovering their authentic paths while contributing to the collective evolution of consciousness. Her work stands as a testament to what becomes possible when spiritual wisdom meets scientific rigor and when profound personal transformation serves the healing of our world.

# RECOMMENDED RESOURCES

## For a Deeper Study of the Four Worlds

### Books on Consciousness and Integration:
- Books by Dr. Eleanor®
  https://nobleenergywellness.com/bookstore/
- Somatic experiencing and body-based psychology
- Contemplative psychology and mindfulness research
- Works by Carl Jung on individuation and the

### Practices for Integration:
- Transcendental Meditation for Spiritual/Archetypal Connection
- Tai Chi or Qigong for embodied integration
- Active imagination and depth psychology approaches
- Clean language and symbolic modeling techniques

### Scientific Research:
- Noble Energy Maps® www.nobleenergymaps.com
- Reading with Dr. Eleanor®
- Consciousness studies and transpersonal psychology
- Neuroscience of meditation and contemplative practice
- Polyvagal theory and nervous system regulation

## Supportive Practices

### Movement and Embodiment:
- Tai Chi Gung with figure-eight patterns
- Yoga practices that integrate breath and movement
- Dance/movement therapy
- Walking meditation and nature connection

### Emotional Processing:
- Somatic experiencing approaches
- Emotional Freedom Technique (EFT)
- Breathwork and pranayama practices
- Sedona Method Releasing

### Mental Clarity:
- Mindfulness and present-moment awareness practices
- Byron Katie's inquiry method
- Sedona Method for releasing limiting beliefs

## Cognitive approaches that serve spiritual development

### Spiritual Connection:
- Contemplative prayer and meditation
- Nature-based spiritual practices
- Service and compassion practices
- Study of perennial wisdom traditions

## Communities and Support

### Finding Like-Minded Others:
- Local meditation and spiritual groups
- Consciousness and integral development communities
- Holistic health and wellness centers
- Online forums for conscious living and spiritual development

### Professional Support:
- Therapists trained in transpersonal or integral approaches
- Spiritual directors and wisdom teachers
- Bodyworkers who understand energy and consciousness
- Medical practitioners who honor the mind-body-spirit connection

## Creating Your Own Curriculum

The most critical resource is your inner wisdom and direct experience. Use external teachings, practices, and communities to support your authentic discovery rather than as authorities to follow blindly.

*Remember Dr. Eleanor's guidance: "You live in your soul; you don't live in your mind." Trust your Knowing, honor your unique path, and allow these resources to serve your authentic unfoldment rather than defining it.*

To learn more about Dr. Eleanor's work, contact her at ehp@noblesciences.com.

To get Dr. Eleanor's Four World Assessment and send it to her, go to: https://nobleenergywellness.com/four-worlds-self-assessment/

www.ingramcontent.com/pod-product-compliance
Lightning Source LLC
Chambersburg PA
CBHW070240090526
44586CB00035B/1360